An Ess Criticism

CW00458581

By
Alexander Pope

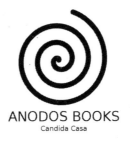

ANODOS BOOKS
Candida Casa

Alexander Pope (1688-1744)
Originally published in 1711
Editing, cover, and internal design by Alisdair MacNoravaich for Anodos Books.
Copyright © 2017 Anodos Books. All rights reserved.

Anodos Books
1c Kings Road
Whithorn
Newton Stewart
Dumfries & Galloway
DG8 8PP

Contents

ALEXANDER POPE.

This eminent English poet was born in London, May 21, 1688. His parents were Roman Catholics, and to this faith the poet adhered, thus debarring himself from public office and employment. His father, a linen merchant, having saved a moderate competency, withdrew from business, and settled on a small estate he had purchased in Windsor Forest. He died at Chiswick, in 1717. His son shortly afterwards took a long lease of a house and five acres of land at Twickenham, on the banks of the Thames, whither he retired with his widowed mother, to whom he was tenderly attached and where he resided till death, cultivating his little domain with exquisite taste and skill, and embellishing it with a grotto, temple, wilderness, and other adjuncts poetical and picturesque. In this famous villa Pope was visited by the most celebrated wits, statesmen and beauties of the day, himself being the most popular and successful poet of his age. His early years were spent at Binfield, within the range of the Royal Forest. He received some education at little Catholic schools, but was his own instructor after his twelfth year. He never was a profound or accurate scholar, but he read Latin poets with ease and delight, and acquired some Greek, French, and Italian. He was a poet almost from infancy, he "lisped in numbers," and when a mere youth surpassed all his contemporaries in metrical harmony and correctness. His pastorals and some translations appeared in 1709, but were written three or four years earlier. These were followed by the *Essay on Criticism*, 1711; *Rape of the Lock* (when completed, the most graceful, airy, and imaginative of his works), 1712-1714; *Windsor Forest*, 1713; *Temple of Fame*, 1715. In a collection of his works printed in 1717 he included the *Epistle of Eloisa* and *Elegy on an Unfortunate Lady*, two poems inimitable for pathetic beauty and finished melodious versification.

From 1715 till 1726 Pope was chiefly engaged on his translations of the *Iliad* and *Odyssey*, which, though wanting in time Homeric simplicity, naturalness, and grandeur, are splendid poems. In 1728-29 he published his greatest satire—the *Dunciad*, an attack on all poetasters and pretended wits, and on all other persons against whom the sensitive poet had conceived any enmity. In 1737 he gave to the world a volume of his *Literary Correspondence*, containing some pleasant gossip and observations, with choice passages of description but it appears that the correspondence was manufactured for publication not composed of actual letters addressed to the parties whose names are given, and the collection was introduced to the public by means of an elaborate stratagem on the part of the scheming poet. Between the years 1731 and 1739 he issued a series of poetical essays moral and philosophical, with satires and imitations of Horace, all admirable for sense, wit, spirit and brilliancy of these delightful productions, the most celebrated is the *Essay on Man* to which

Bolingbroke is believed to have contributed the spurious philosophy and false sentiment, but its merit consists in detached passages, descriptions, and pictures. A fourth book to the *Dunciad*, containing many beautiful and striking lines and a general revision of his works, closed the poet's literary cares and toils. He died on the 30th of May, 1744, and was buried in the church at Twickenham.

Pope was of very diminutive stature and deformed from his birth. His physical infirmity, susceptible temperament, and incessant study rendered his life one long disease. He was, as his friend Lord Chesterfield said, "the most irritable of all the *genus irritabile vatum*, offended with trifles and never forgetting or forgiving them." His literary stratagems, disguises, assertions, denials, and (we must add) misrepresentations would fill volumes. Yet when no disturbing jealousy vanity, or rivalry intervened was generous and affectionate, and he had a manly, independent spirit. As a poet he was deficient in originality and creative power, and thus was inferior to his prototype, Dryden, but as a literary artist, and brilliant declaimer satirist and moralizer in verse he is still unrivaled. He is the English Horace, and will as surely descend with honors to the latest posterity.

PART I.

'Tis hard to say if greater want of skill
Appear in writing or in judging ill,
But of the two less dangerous is the offense
To tire our patience than mislead our sense
5   Some few in that but numbers err in this,
Ten censure wrong for one who writes amiss,
A fool might once himself alone expose,
Now one in verse makes many more in prose.

'Tis with our judgments as our watches, none
10   Go just alike, yet each believes his own
In poets as true genius is but rare
True taste as seldom is the critic share
Both must alike from Heaven derive their light,
These born to judge as well as those to write
15   Let such teach others who themselves excel,
And censure freely, who have written well
Authors are partial to their wit, 'tis true[1]
But are not critics to their judgment too?

Yet if we look more closely we shall find
20   Most have the seeds of judgment in their mind
Nature affords at least a glimmering light
The lines though touched but faintly are drawn right,
But as the slightest sketch if justly traced
Is by ill coloring but the more disgraced
25   So by false learning is good sense defaced
Some are bewildered in the maze of schools[2]
And some made coxcombs nature meant but fools
In search of wit these lose their common sense
And then turn critics in their own defense
30   Each burns alike who can or cannot write
Or with a rival's or an eunuch's spite
All fools have still an itching to deride
And fain would be upon the laughing side
If Maevius scribble in Apollo's spite[3]
35   There are who judge still worse than he can write.

---

[1]**Wit** is used in the poem in a great variety of meanings (1) Here it seems to mean *genius* or *fancy*, (2) in line 36 *a man of fancy*, (3) in line 53 *the understanding* or *powers of the mind*, (4) in line 81 it means *judgment*.

[2]**Schools**—Different systems of doctrine or philosophy as taught by particular teachers.

[3]**Maevius**—An insignificant poet of the Augustan age, ridiculed by Virgil in his third Eclogue and by Horace in his tenth Epode.

Some have at first for wits then poets passed
Turned critics next and proved plain fools at last
Some neither can for wits nor critics pass
As heavy mules are neither horse nor ass.
40   Those half-learned witlings, numerous in our isle,
As half-formed insects on the banks of Nile
Unfinished things one knows not what to call
Their generation is so equivocal
To tell them would a hundred tongues require,
45   Or one vain wits that might a hundred tire.

But you who seek to give and merit fame,
And justly bear a critic's noble name,
Be sure yourself and your own reach to know
How far your genius taste and learning go.
50   Launch not beyond your depth, but be discreet
And mark that point where sense and dullness meet.

Nature to all things fixed the limits fit
And wisely curbed proud man's pretending wit.
As on the land while here the ocean gains.
55   In other parts it leaves wide sandy plains
Thus in the soul while memory prevails,
The solid power of understanding fails
Where beams of warm imagination play,
The memory's soft figures melt away
60   One science only will one genius fit,
So vast is art, so narrow human wit
Not only bounded to peculiar arts,
But oft in those confined to single parts
Like kings, we lose the conquests gained before,
65   By vain ambition still to make them more
Each might his several province well command,
Would all but stoop to what they understand.

First follow nature and your judgment frame
By her just standard, which is still the same.
70   Unerring nature still divinely bright,
One clear, unchanged and universal light,
Life force and beauty, must to all impart,
At once the source and end and test of art
Art from that fund each just supply provides,
75   Works without show and without pomp presides
In some fair body thus the informing soul
With spirits feeds, with vigor fills the whole,
Each motion guides and every nerve sustains,
Itself unseen, but in the effects remains.

80　Some, to whom Heaven in wit has been profuse,[4]
　　Want as much more, to turn it to its use;
　　For wit and judgment often are at strife,
　　Though meant each other's aid, like man and wife.
　　'Tis more to guide, than spur the muse's steed,
85　Restrain his fury, than provoke his speed,
　　The winged courser, like a generous horse,[5]
　　Shows most true mettle when you check his course.

　　Those rules, of old discovered, not devised,
　　Are nature still, but nature methodized;
90　Nature, like liberty, is but restrained
　　By the same laws which first herself ordained.

　　Hear how learned Greece her useful rules indites,
　　When to repress and when indulge our flights.
　　High on Parnassus' top her sons she showed,[6]
95　And pointed out those arduous paths they trod;
　　Held from afar, aloft, the immortal prize,
　　And urged the rest by equal steps to rise.[7]
　　Just precepts thus from great examples given,
　　She drew from them what they derived from Heaven.
100　The generous critic fanned the poet's fire,
　　And taught the world with reason to admire.
　　Then criticism the muse's handmaid proved,
　　To dress her charms, and make her more beloved:
　　But following wits from that intention strayed
105　Who could not win the mistress, wooed the maid
　　Against the poets their own arms they turned
　　Sure to hate most the men from whom they learned
　　So modern 'pothecaries taught the art
　　By doctors bills to play the doctor's part.
110　Bold in the practice of mistaken rules
　　Prescribe, apply, and call their masters fools.
　　Some on the leaves of ancient authors prey,
　　Nor time nor moths e'er spoil so much as they.

---

[4]There is here a slight inaccuracy or inconsistency, since "wit" has a different meaning in the two lines: in 80, it means *fancy*, in 81, *judgment*.

[5]**The winged courser.**—Pegasus, a winged horse which sprang from the blood of Medusa when Perseus cut off her head. As soon as born he left the earth and flew up to heaven, or, according to Ovid, took up his abode on Mount Helicon, and was always associated with the Muses.

[6]**Parnassus.**—A mountain of Phocis, which received its name from Parnassus, the son of Neptune, and was sacred to the Muses, Apollo and Bacchus.

[7]**Equal steps.**—Steps equal to the undertaking.

Some dryly plain, without invention's aid,
115 Write dull receipts how poems may be made
These leave the sense their learning to display,
And those explain the meaning quite away.

You then, whose judgment the right course would steer,
Know well each ancient's proper character,
120 His fable subject scope in every page,
Religion, country, genius of his age
Without all these at once before your eyes,
Cavil you may, but never criticise.
Be Homers works your study and delight,
125 Read them by day and meditate by night,
Thence form your judgment thence your maxims bring
And trace the muses upward to their spring.
Still with itself compared, his text peruse,
And let your comment be the Mantuan Muse.[8]

130 When first young Maro in his boundless mind,[9]
A work to outlast immortal Rome designed,
Perhaps he seemed above the critic's law
And but from nature's fountain scorned to draw
But when to examine every part he came
135 Nature and Homer were he found the same
Convinced, amazed, he checks the bold design
And rules as strict his labored work confine
As if the Stagirite o'erlooked each line[10]
Learn hence for ancient rules a just esteem,
140 To copy nature is to copy them.

---

[8]**The Mantuan Muse**—Virgil called Maro in the next line (his full name being, Virgilius Publius Maro) born near Mantua, 70 B.C.

[9]It is said that Virgil first intended to write a poem on the Alban and Roman affairs which he found beyond his powers, and then he imitated Homer:

Cum canerem reges et proelia Cynthius aurem
Vellit—*Virg. Ecl. VI*

[10]**The Stagirite**—Aristotle, born at the Greek town of Stageira on the Strymonic Gulf (Gulf of Contessa, in Turkey) 384 B.C., whose treatises on Rhetoric and the Art of Poetry were the earliest development of a Philosophy of Criticism and still continue to be studied.

The poet contradicts himself with regard to the principle he is here laying down in lines 271-272 where he laughs at Dennis for

Concluding all were desperate sots and fools
Who durst depart from Aristotle's rules.

Some beauties yet no precepts can declare,
For there's a happiness as well as care.
Music resembles poetry—in each
Are nameless graces which no methods teach,
145 And which a master hand alone can reach
If, where the rules not far enough extend
(Since rules were made but to promote their end),
Some lucky license answer to the full
The intent proposed that license is a rule.
150 Thus Pegasus a nearer way to take
May boldly deviate from the common track
Great wits sometimes may gloriously offend,
And rise to faults true critics dare not mend,
From vulgar bounds with brave disorder part,
155 And snatch a grace beyond the reach of art,
Which without passing through the judgment gains
The heart and all its end at once attains.
In prospects, thus, some objects please our eyes,
Which out of nature's common order rise,
160 The shapeless rock or hanging precipice.
But though the ancients thus their rules invade
(As kings dispense with laws themselves have made),
Moderns beware! or if you must offend
Against the precept, ne'er transgress its end,
165 Let it be seldom, and compelled by need,
And have, at least, their precedent to plead.
The critic else proceeds without remorse,
Seizes your fame, and puts his laws in force.

I know there are, to whose presumptuous thoughts
170 Those freer beauties, even in them, seem faults
Some figures monstrous and misshaped appear,
Considered singly, or beheld too near,
Which, but proportioned to their light, or place,
Due distance reconciles to form and grace.
175 A prudent chief not always must display
His powers in equal ranks and fair array,
But with the occasion and the place comply.
Conceal his force, nay, seem sometimes to fly.
Those oft are stratagems which errors seem,
180 Nor is it Homer nods, but we that dream.[11]

Still green with bays each ancient altar stands,
Above the reach of sacrilegious hands,

---

[11]**Homer nods**—*Quandoque bonus dormitat Homerus*, 'even the good Homer nods'—Horace, *Epistola ad Pisones*, 359.

7

Secure from flames, from envy's fiercer rage,[12]
Destructive war, and all-involving age.
185 See, from each clime the learned their incense bring;
Hear, in all tongues consenting Paeans ring!
In praise so just let every voice be joined,
And fill the general chorus of mankind.
Hail! bards triumphant! born in happier days;
190 Immortal heirs of universal praise!
Whose honors with increase of ages grow,
As streams roll down, enlarging as they flow;
Nations unborn your mighty names shall sound,[13]
And worlds applaud that must not yet be found!
195 Oh may some spark of your celestial fire,
The last, the meanest of your sons inspire,
(That, on weak wings, from far pursues your flights,
Glows while he reads, but trembles as he writes),
To teach vain wits a science little known,
200 To admire superior sense, and doubt their own!

---

[12]**Secure from flames**.—The poet probably alludes to such fires as those in which the Alexandrine and Palatine Libraries were destroyed. **From envy's fiercer rage**.—Probably he alludes to the writings of such men as Maevius (see note to line 34) and Zoilus, a sophist and grammarian of Amphipolis, who distinguished himself by his criticism on Isocrates, Plato, and Homer, receiving the nickname of *Homeromastic* (chastiser of Homer). **Destructive war**— Probably an allusion to the irruption of the barbarians into the south of Europe. **And all-involving age**; that is, time. This is usually explained as an allusion to 'the long reign of ignorance and superstition in the cloisters,' but it is surely far-fetched, and more than the language will bear.

[13]'Round the whole world this dreaded name shall sound,
And reach to worlds that must not yet be found,"—COWLEY.

PART II.

Of all the causes which conspire to blind
Man's erring judgment and misguide the mind,
What the weak head with strongest bias rules,
Is pride, the never-failing vice of fools.
205 Whatever nature has in worth denied,
She gives in large recruits of needful pride;
For as in bodies, thus in souls, we find
What wants in blood and spirits, swelled with wind:
Pride where wit fails steps in to our defense,
210 And fills up all the mighty void of sense.
If once right reason drives that cloud away,
Truth breaks upon us with resistless day
Trust not yourself, but your defects to know,
Make use of every friend—and every foe.

215 A little learning is a dangerous thing
Drink deep, or taste not the Pierian spring[14]
There shallow draughts intoxicate the brain,
And drinking largely sobers us again.
Fired at first sight with what the muse imparts,
220 In fearless youth we tempt the heights of arts
While from the bounded level of our mind
Short views we take nor see the lengths behind
But more advanced behold with strange surprise,
New distant scenes of endless science rise!
225 So pleased at first the towering Alps we try,
Mount o'er the vales and seem to tread the sky,
The eternal snows appear already passed
And the first clouds and mountains seem the last.
But those attained we tremble to survey
230 The growing labors of the lengthened way
The increasing prospect tires our wandering eyes,
Hills peep o'er hills and Alps on Alps arise!

A perfect judge will read each work of wit
With the same spirit that its author writ
235 Survey the whole nor seek slight faults to find
Where nature moves and rapture warms the mind,
Nor lose for that malignant dull delight
The generous pleasure to be charmed with wit
But in such lays as neither ebb nor flow,
240 Correctly cold and regularly low

---

[14]**The Pierian spring**—A fountain in Pieria, a district round Mount Olympus and the native country of the Muses.

That, shunning faults, one quiet tenor keep;
We cannot blame indeed—but we may sleep.
In wit, as nature, what affects our hearts
Is not the exactness of peculiar parts,
245 'Tis not a lip, or eye, we beauty call,
But the joint force and full result of all.
Thus, when we view some well proportioned dome
(The worlds just wonder, and even thine, O Rome!),[15]
No single parts unequally surprise,
250 All comes united to the admiring eyes;
No monstrous height or breadth, or length, appear;
The whole at once is bold, and regular.

Whoever thinks a faultless piece to see.
Thinks what ne'er was, nor is, nor e'er shall be.
255 In every work regard the writer's end,
Since none can compass more than they intend;
And if the means be just, the conduct true,
Applause, in spite of trivial faults, is due.
As men of breeding, sometimes men of wit,
260 To avoid great errors, must the less commit:
Neglect the rules each verbal critic lays,
For not to know some trifles is a praise.
Most critics, fond of some subservient art,
Still make the whole depend upon a part:
265 They talk of principles, but notions prize,
And all to one loved folly sacrifice.

Once on a time La Mancha's knight, they say,[16]
A certain bard encountering on the way,
Discoursed in terms as just, with looks as sage,
270 As e'er could Dennis, of the Grecian stage;[17]
Concluding all were desperate sots and fools,
Who durst depart from Aristotle's rules
Our author, happy in a judge so nice,
Produced his play, and begged the knight's advice;

---

[15]**And even thine, O Rome.**—The dome of St Peter's Church, designed by Michael Angelo.

[16]**La Mancha's Knight.**—Don Quixote, a fictitious Spanish knight, the hero of a book written (1605) by Cervantes, a Spanish writer.

[17]**Dennis,** the son of a saddler in London, born 1657, was a mediocre writer, and rather better critic of the time, with whom Pope came a good deal into collision. Addison's tragedy of *Cato*, for which Pope had written a prologue, had been attacked by Dennis. Pope, to defend Addison, wrote an imaginary report, pretending to be written by a notorious quack mad-doctor of the day, entitled *The Narrative of Dr. Robert Norris on the Frenz of F. D.* Dennis replied to it by his Character *of Mr. Pope.* Ultimately Pope gave him a place in his *Dunciad*, and wrote a prologue for his benefit.]

275 Made him observe the subject, and the plot,
The manners, passions, unities, what not?
All which, exact to rule, were brought about,
Were but a combat in the lists left out
"What! leave the combat out?" exclaims the knight.
280 "Yes, or we must renounce the Stagirite."
"Not so, by heaven!" (he answers in a rage)
"Knights, squires, and steeds must enter on the stage."
"So vast a throng the stage can ne'er contain."
"Then build a new, or act it in a plain."

285 Thus critics of less judgment than caprice,
Curious, not knowing, not exact, but nice,
Form short ideas, and offend in arts
(As most in manners) by a love to parts.

Some to conceit alone their taste confine,
290 And glittering thoughts struck out at every line;
Pleased with a work where nothing's just or fit;
One glaring chaos and wild heap of wit.
Poets, like painters, thus, unskilled to trace
The naked nature and the living grace,
295 With gold and jewels cover every part,
And hide with ornaments their want of art.
True wit is nature to advantage dressed;
What oft was thought, but ne'er so well expressed;
Something, whose truth convinced at sight we find
300 That gives us back the image of our mind.
As shades more sweetly recommend the light,
So modest plainness sets off sprightly wit
For works may have more wit than does them good,
As bodies perish through excess of blood.

305 Others for language all their care express,
And value books, as women men, for dress.
Their praise is still—"the style is excellent,"
The sense they humbly take upon content[18]
Words are like leaves, and where they most abound
310 Much fruit of sense beneath is rarely found.
False eloquence, like the prismatic glass.[19]
Its gaudy colors spreads on every place,
The face of nature we no more survey.

---

[18]**On content**.—On trust, a common use of the word in Pope's time.

[19]**Prismatic glass**.—A glass prism by which light is refracted, and the component rays, which are of different colors being refracted at different angles show what is called a spectrum or series of colored bars, in the order violet, indigo, blue, green, yellow, orange, red.

All glares alike without distinction gay:
315 But true expression, like the unchanging sun,
Clears and improves whate'er it shines upon;
It gilds all objects, but it alters none.
Expression is the dress of thought, and still
Appears more decent, as more suitable,
320 A vile conceit in pompous words expressed,
Is like a clown in regal purple dressed
For different styles with different subjects sort,
As several garbs with country town and court
Some by old words to fame have made pretense,
325 Ancients in phrase, mere moderns in their sense;
Such labored nothings, in so strange a style,
Amaze the unlearned, and make the learned smile.
Unlucky, as Fungoso in the play,[20]
These sparks with awkward vanity display
330 What the fine gentleman wore yesterday;
And but so mimic ancient wits at best,
As apes our grandsires in their doublets dressed.
In words as fashions the same rule will hold,
Alike fantastic if too new or old.
335 Be not the first by whom the new are tried,
Nor yet the last to lay the old aside

But most by numbers judge a poet's song
And smooth or rough, with them is right or wrong.
In the bright muse though thousand charms conspire,
340 Her voice is all these tuneful fools admire,
Who haunt Parnassus but to please their ear,
Not mend their minds, as some to church repair,
Not for the doctrine but the music there
These equal syllables alone require,
345 Though oft the ear the open vowels tire;
While expletives their feeble aid do join;
And ten low words oft creep in one dull line,
While they ring round the same unvaried chimes,
With sure returns of still expected rhymes,
350 Where'er you find "the cooling western breeze,"
In the next line it "whispers through the trees"
If crystal streams "with pleasing murmurs creep"
The reader's threatened (not in vain) with "sleep"
Then, at the last and only couplet fraught
355 With some unmeaning thing they call a thought,

---

[20]**Fungoso**—One of the characters in Ben Jonson's *Every Man out of his Humor* who assumed the dress and tried to pass himself off for another.

13

A needless Alexandrine ends the song[21]
That, like a wounded snake drags its slow length along.

Leave such to tune their own dull rhymes, and know
What's roundly smooth or languishingly slow;
360 And praise the easy vigor of a line,
Where Denham's strength, and Waller's sweetness join.[22]
True ease in writing comes from art, not chance,
As those move easiest who have learned to dance
'Tis not enough no harshness gives offense,
365 The sound must seem an echo to the sense.
Soft is the strain when Zephyr gently blows,[23]
And the smooth stream in smoother numbers flows,
But when loud surges lash the sounding shore,
The hoarse, rough verse should like the torrent roar,
370 When Ajax strives some rock's vast weight to throw,
The line too labors, and the words move slow;
Not so, when swift Camilla scours the plain,
Flies o'er the unbending corn, and skims along the main.[24]

---

[21]**Alexandrine**—A line of twelve syllables, so called from a French poem on the Life of Alexander the Great, written in that meter. The poet gives a remarkable example in the next line.

[22]Sir John Denham, a poet of the time of Charles I. (1615-1668). His verse is characterized by considerable smoothness and ingenuity of rhythm, with here and there a passage of some force —Edmund Waller (1606-1687) is celebrated as one of the refiners of English poetry. His rank among English poets, however, is very subordinate.

[23]**Zephyr.**—Zephyrus, the west wind personified by the poets and made the most mild and gentle of the sylvan deities.

[24]In this passage the poet obviously intended to make "the sound seem an echo to the sense". The success of the attempt has not been very complete except in the second two lines, expressing the dash and roar of the waves, and in the last two, expressing the skimming, continuous motion of Camilla. What he refers to is the onomatopoeia of Homer and Virgil in the passages alluded to. **Ajax**, the son of Telamon, was, next to Achilles, the bravest of all the Greeks in the Trojan war. When the Greeks were challenged by Hector he was chosen their champion and it was in their encounter that he seized a huge stone and hurled it at Hector.

Thus rendered by Pope himself:

"Then Ajax seized the fragment of a rock
Applied each nerve, and swinging round on high,
With force tempestuous let the ruin fly
The huge stone thundering through his buckler broke."

Camilla, queen of the Volsci, was brought up in the woods, and, according to Virgil, was swifter than the winds. She led an army to assist Turnus against Aeneas.

Hear how Timotheus' varied lays surprise,[25]
375 And bid alternate passions fall and rise!
While, at each change, the son of Libyan Jove[26]
Now burns with glory, and then melts with love;
Now his fierce eyes with sparkling fury glow,
Now sighs steal out, and tears begin to flow:
380 Persians and Greeks like turns of nature found,
And the world's victor stood subdued by sound?
The power of music all our hearts allow,
And what Timotheus was, is Dryden now.

Avoid extremes, and shun the fault of such,
385 Who still are pleased too little or too much.
At every trifle scorn to take offense,
That always shows great pride, or little sense:
Those heads, as stomachs, are not sure the best,
Which nauseate all, and nothing can digest.
390 Yet let not each gay turn thy rapture move;
For fools admire, but men of sense approve:
As things seem large which we through mist descry,
Dullness is ever apt to magnify.[27]

Some foreign writers, some our own despise,
395 The ancients only, or the moderns prize.
Thus wit, like faith, by each man is applied
To one small sect, and all are damned beside.

"Dura pan, cursuque pedum praevertere ventos.
Illa vel intactae segetis per summa volaret
Gramina nec teneras cursu laesisset aristas;
Vel mare per medium fluctu suspensa tumenti,
Ferret iter, celeres nec tingeret aequore plantas."
Aen. vii 807-811.

Thus rendered by Dryden.

"Outstripped the winds in speed upon the plain,
Flew o'er the fields, nor hurt the bearded grain;
She swept the seas, and as she skimmed along,
Her flying feet unbathed on billows hung"

[25]This passage refers to Dryden's ode, *Alexander's Feast*, or *The Power of Music*. Timotheus, mentioned in it, was a musician of Boeotia, a favorite of Alexander's, not the great musician Timotheus, who died before Alexander was born, unless, indeed, Dryden have confused the two.

[26]**The son of Libyan Jove.**—A title arrogated to himself by Alexander.

[27]**Dullness** here 'seems to be incorrectly used. Ignorance is apt to magnify, but dullness reposes in stolid indifference.'

Meanly they seek the blessing to confine,
And force that sun but on a part to shine,
400 Which not alone the southern wit sublimes,
But ripens spirits in cold northern climes.
Which from the first has shone on ages past,
Enlights the present, and shall warm the last,
Though each may feel increases and decays,
405 And see now clearer and now darker days.
Regard not then if wit be old or new,
But blame the false, and value still the true.

Some ne'er advance a judgment of their own,
But catch the spreading notion of the town,
410 They reason and conclude by precedent,
And own stale nonsense which they ne'er invent.
Some judge of authors names not works, and then
Nor praise nor blame the writing, but the men.
Of all this servile herd the worst is he
415 That in proud dullness joins with quality
A constant critic at the great man's board,
To fetch and carry nonsense for my lord
What woful stuff this madrigal would be,
In some starved hackney sonnetteer, or me!
420 But let a lord once own the happy lines,
How the wit brightens! how the style refines!
Before his sacred name flies every fault,
And each exalted stanza teems with thought!

The vulgar thus through imitation err;
425 As oft the learned by being singular.
So much they scorn the crowd that if the throng
By chance go right they purposely go wrong:
So schismatics the plain believers quit,
And are but damned for having too much wit.
430 Some praise at morning what they blame at night,
But always think the last opinion right.
A muse by these is like a mistress used,
This hour she's idolized, the next abused;
While their weak heads, like towns unfortified,
435 'Twixt sense and nonsense daily change their side.
Ask them the cause, they're wiser still they say;
And still to-morrow's wiser than to-day.
We think our fathers fools, so wise we grow;
Our wiser sons, no doubt, will think us so.
440 Once school-divines this zealous isle o'erspread.

Who knew most sentences was deepest read,[28]
Faith, Gospel, all, seemed made to be disputed,
And none had sense enough to be confuted:
Scotists and Thomists now in peace remain,[29]
445 Amidst their kindred cobwebs in Duck Lane.[30]
If faith itself has different dresses worn,
What wonder modes in wit should take their turn?
Oft, leaving what is natural and fit,
The current folly proves the ready wit;
450 And authors think their reputation safe,
Which lives as long as fools are pleased to laugh.

Some valuing those of their own side or mind,
Still make themselves the measure of mankind:
Fondly we think we honor merit then,
455 When we but praise ourselves in other men.
Parties in wit attend on those of state,
And public faction doubles private hate.
Pride, malice, folly against Dryden rose,
In various shapes of parsons, critics, beaux;[31]
460 But sense survived, when merry jests were past;
For rising merit will buoy up at last.
Might he return, and bless once more our eyes,
New Blackmores and new Millbourns must arise:[32]
Nay, should great Homer lift his awful head,

---

[28]**Sentences**—Passages from the Fathers of the Church who were regarded as decisive authorities on all disputed points of doctrine.

[29]**Scotists**—The disciples of Duns Scotus, one of the most famous and influential of the scholastics of the fourteenth century, who was opposed to Thomas Aquinas (1224-1274), another famous scholastic, regarding the doctrines of grace and the freedom of the will, but especially the immaculate conception of the Virgin. The followers of the latter were called Thomists, between whom and the Scotists bitter controversies were carried on.

[30]**Duck Lane**.—A place near Smithfield where old books were sold. The cobwebs were kindred to the works of these controversialists, because their arguments were intricate and obscure. Scotus is said to have demolished two hundred objections to the doctrine of the immaculate conception, and established it by a cloud of proofs.

[31]**Parsons**.—This is an allusion to Jeremy Collier, the author of *A Short View etc, of the English Stage*. **Critics, beaux**.—This to the Duke of Buckingham, the author of *The Rehearsal*.

[32]**Blackmore**, Sir Richard (1652-1729), one of the court physicians and the writer of a great deal of worthless poetry. He attacked the dramatists of the time generally and Dryden individually, and is the Quack Maurus of Dryden's prologue to *The Secular Masque*. **Millbourn**, Rev. Luke, who criticised Dryden; which criticism, although sneered at by Pope, is allowed to have been judicious and decisive.

465 Zoilus again would start up from the dead[33]
Envy will merit, as its shade, pursue,
But like a shadow, proves the substance true:
For envied wit, like Sol eclipsed, makes known
The opposing body's grossness, not its own.
470 When first that sun too powerful beams displays,
It draws up vapors which obscure its rays,
But even those clouds at last adorn its way
Reflect new glories and augment the day

Be thou the first true merit to befriend
475 His praise is lost who stays till all commend
Short is the date alas! of modern rhymes
And 'tis but just to let them live betimes
No longer now that golden age appears
When patriarch wits survived a thousand years[34]
480 Now length of fame (our second life) is lost
And bare threescore is all even that can boast,
Our sons their fathers failing language see
And such as Chaucer is shall Dryden be
So when the faithful pencil has designed
485 Some bright idea of the master's mind
Where a new world leaps out at his command
And ready nature waits upon his hand
When the ripe colors soften and unite
And sweetly melt into just shade and light
490 When mellowing years their full perfection give
And each bold figure just begins to live
The treacherous colors the fair art betray
And all the bright creation fades away!

Unhappy wit, like most mistaken things
495 Atones not for that envy which it brings
In youth alone its empty praise we boast
But soon the short lived vanity is lost.
Like some fair flower the early spring supplies
That gayly blooms but even in blooming dies
500 What is this wit, which must our cares employ?
The owner's wife that other men enjoy
Then most our trouble still when most admired
And still the more we give the more required
Whose fame with pains we guard, but lose with ease,
505 Sure some to vex, but never all to please,

---

[33]**Zoilus**. See note on line 183.

[34]**Patriarch wits**—Perhaps an allusion to the great age to which the antediluvian patriarchs of the Bible lived.

18

'Tis what the vicious fear, the virtuous shun,
By fools 'tis hated, and by knaves undone!

If wit so much from ignorance undergo,
Ah! let not learning too commence its foe!
510   Of old, those met rewards who could excel,
And such were praised who but endeavored well:
Though triumphs were to generals only due,
Crowns were reserved to grace the soldiers too.
Now they who reach Parnassus' lofty crown,
515   Employ their pains to spurn some others down;
And, while self-love each jealous writer rules,
Contending wits become the sport of fools:
But still the worst with most regret commend,
For each ill author is as bad a friend
520   To what base ends, and by what abject ways,
Are mortals urged, through sacred lust of praise!
Ah, ne'er so dire a thirst of glory boast,
Nor in the critic let the man be lost
Good-nature and good sense must ever join;
525   To err is human, to forgive, divine.

But if in noble minds some dregs remain,
Not yet purged off, of spleen and sour disdain;
Discharge that rage on more provoking crimes,
Nor fear a dearth in these flagitious times.
530   No pardon vile obscenity should find,
Though wit and art conspire to move your mind;
But dullness with obscenity must prove
As shameful sure as impotence in love.
In the fat age of pleasure, wealth, and ease,
535   Sprung the rank weed, and thrived with large increase:
When love was all an easy monarch's care,[35]
Seldom at council, never in a war
Jilts ruled the state, and statesmen farces writ;
Nay, wits had pensions, and young lords had wit:
540   The fair sat panting at a courtier's play,
And not a mask went unimproved away:[36]
The modest fan was lifted up no more,
And virgins smiled at what they blushed before.
The following license of a foreign reign,[37]

---

[35]**An easy monarch**.—Charles II.

[36]At that time ladies went to the theater in masks.

[37]**A foreign reign**.—The reign of the foreigner, William III.

545 Did all the dregs of bold Socinus drain,[38]
Then unbelieving priests reformed the nation.
And taught more pleasant methods of salvation;
Where Heaven's free subjects might their rights dispute,
Lest God himself should seem too absolute:
550 Pulpits their sacred satire learned to spare,
And vice admired to find a flatterer there!
Encouraged thus, wit's Titans braved the skies,[39]
And the press groaned with licensed blasphemies.
These monsters, critics! with your darts engage,
555 Here point your thunder, and exhaust your rage!
Yet shun their fault, who, scandalously nice,
Will needs mistake an author into vice;
All seems infected that the infected spy,
As all looks yellow to the jaundiced eye.

---

[38]**Socinus.**—The reaction from the fanaticism of the Puritans, who held extreme notions of free grace and satisfaction, by resolving all Christianity into morality, led the way to the introduction of Socinianism, the most prominent feature of which is the denial of the existence of the Trinity.

[39]**Wit's Titans.**—The Titans, in Greek mythology, were the children of Uranus (heaven) and Gaea (earth), and of gigantic size. They engaged in a conflict with Zeus, the king of heaven, which lasted ten years. They were completely defeated, and hurled down into a dungeon below Tartarus. Very often they are confounded with the Giants, as has apparently been done here by Pope. These were a later progeny of the same parents, and in revenge for what had been done to the Titans, conspired to dethrone Zeus. In order to scale heaven, they piled Mount Ossa upon Pelion, and would have succeeded in their attempt if Zeus had not called in the assistance of his son Hercules.

PART III.

560   Learn, then, what morals critics ought to show,
For 'tis but half a judge's task to know.
'Tis not enough, taste, judgment, learning, join;
In all you speak, let truth and candor shine:
That not alone what to your sense is due
565   All may allow, but seek your friendship too.

Be silent always, when you doubt your sense;
And speak, though sure, with seeming diffidence:
Some positive persisting fops we know,
Who, if once wrong will needs be always so;
570   But you, with pleasure, own your errors past,
And make each day a critique on the last.

'Tis not enough your counsel still be true;
Blunt truths more mischief than nice falsehoods do;
Men must be taught as if you taught them not,
575   And things unknown proposed as things forgot.
Without good breeding truth is disapproved;
That only makes superior sense beloved.

Be niggards of advice on no pretense;
For the worst avarice is that of sense
580   With mean complacence, ne'er betray your trust,
Nor be so civil as to prove unjust
Fear not the anger of the wise to raise,
Those best can bear reproof who merit praise.

'Twere well might critics still this freedom take,
585   But Appius reddens at each word you speak,[40]
And stares, tremendous with a threatening eye,
Like some fierce tyrant in old tapestry
Fear most to tax an honorable fool
Whose right it is uncensured to be dull
590   Such, without wit are poets when they please,
As without learning they can take degrees
Leave dangerous truths to unsuccessful satires,
And flattery to fulsome dedicators
Whom, when they praise, the world believes no more,
595   Than when they promise to give scribbling o'er.

'Tis best sometimes your censure to restrain,

---

[40]**Appius**.—He refers to Dennis (see note to verse 270) who had published a tragedy called *Appius and Virginia*. He retaliated for these remarks by coarse personalities upon Pope, in his criticism of this poem.

And charitably let the dull be vain
Your silence there is better than your spite,
For who can rail so long as they can write?
600 Still humming on, their drowsy course they keep,
And lashed so long like tops are lashed asleep.
False steps but help them to renew the race,
As after stumbling, jades will mend their pace.
What crowds of these, impenitently bold,
605 In sounds and jingling syllables grown old,
Still run on poets in a raging vein,
Even to the dregs and squeezing of the brain;
Strain out the last dull droppings of their sense,
And rhyme with all the rage of impotence!

610 Such shameless bards we have, and yet, 'tis true,
There are as mad abandoned critics, too
The bookful blockhead ignorantly read,
With loads of learned lumber in his head,
With his own tongue still edifies his ears,
615 And always listening to himself appears
All books he reads and all he reads assails
From Dryden's Fables down to Durfey's Tales[41]
With him most authors steal their works or buy;
Garth did not write his own Dispensary[42]
620 Name a new play, and he's the poets friend
Nay, showed his faults—but when would poets mend?
No place so sacred from such fops is barred,
Nor is Paul's Church more safe than Paul's Churchyard:[43]
Nay, fly to altars; there they'll talk you dead,
625 For fools rush in where angels fear to tread
Distrustful sense with modest caution speaks,
It still looks home, and short excursions makes;
But rattling nonsense in full volleys breaks,
And, never shocked, and never turned aside.
630 Bursts out, resistless, with a thundering tide,

But where's the man who counsel can bestow,

---

[41]**Durfey's Tales.**—Thomas D'Urfey, the author (in the reign of Charles II.) of a sequel in five acts of *The Rehearsal*, a series of sonnets entitled *Pills to Purge Melancholy*, the Tales here alluded to, etc. He was a very inferior poet, although Addison pleaded for him.

[42]**Garth, Dr.**, afterwards Sir Samuel (born 1660) an eminent physician and a poet of considerable reputation He is best known as the author of *The Dispensary*, a poetical satire on the apothecaries and physicians who opposed the project of giving medicine gratuitously to the sick poor. The poet alludes to a slander current at the time with regard to the authorship of the poem.

[43]**St Paul's Churchyard**, before the fire of London, was the headquarters of the booksellers.

Still pleased to teach, and yet not proud to know?
Unbiased, or by favor, or in spite,
Not dully prepossessed, nor blindly right;
635 Though learned, well-bred, and though well bred, sincere,
Modestly bold, and humanly severe,
Who to a friend his faults can freely show,
And gladly praise the merit of a foe?
Blessed with a taste exact, yet unconfined;
640 A knowledge both of books and human kind;
Generous converse, a soul exempt from pride;
And love to praise, with reason on his side?

Such once were critics such the happy few,
Athens and Rome in better ages knew.
645 The mighty Stagirite first left the shore,[44]
Spread all his sails, and durst the deeps explore;
He steered securely, and discovered far,
Led by the light of the Maeonian star.[45]
Poets, a race long unconfined and free,
650 Still fond and proud of savage liberty,
Received his laws, and stood convinced 'twas fit,
Who conquered nature, should preside o'er wit.[46]

Horace still charms with graceful negligence,
And without method talks us into sense;
655 Will like a friend familiarly convey
The truest notions in the easiest way.
He who supreme in judgment as in wit,
Might boldly censure, as he boldly writ,
Yet judged with coolness though he sung with fire;
660 His precepts teach but what his works inspire
Our critics take a contrary extreme
They judge with fury, but they write with phlegm:
Nor suffers Horace more in wrong translations
By wits than critics in as wrong quotations.

665 See Dionysius Homer's thoughts refine,[47]

---

[44]See note on line 138.

[45]**The Maeonian star**.—Homer, supposed by some to have been born in Maeonia, a part of Lydia in Asia Minor, and whose poems were the chief subject of Aristotle's criticism.

[46]**Who conquered nature**—He wrote, besides his other works, treatises on Astronomy, Mechanics, Physics, and Natural History.

[47]**Dionysius**, born at Halicarnassus about 50 B.C., was a learned critic, historian, and rhetorician at Rome in the Augustan age.

And call new beauties forth from every line!

Fancy and art in gay Petronius please,[48]
The scholar's learning with the courtier's ease.

In grave Quintilian's copious work we find[49]
670   The justest rules and clearest method joined:
Thus useful arms in magazines we place,
All ranged in order, and disposed with grace,
But less to please the eye, than arm the hand,
Still fit for use, and ready at command.

675   Thee bold Longinus! all the Nine inspire,[50]
And bless their critic with a poet's fire.
An ardent judge, who, zealous in his trust,
With warmth gives sentence, yet is always just:
Whose own example strengthens all his laws;
680   And is himself that great sublime he draws.

Thus long succeeding critics justly reigned,
License repressed, and useful laws ordained.
Learning and Rome alike in empire grew;
And arts still followed where her eagles flew,
685   From the same foes at last, both felt their doom,
And the same age saw learning fall, and Rome.[51]
With tyranny then superstition joined
As that the body, this enslaved the mind;
Much was believed but little understood,
690   And to be dull was construed to be good;
A second deluge learning thus o'errun,

---

[48]**Petronius.**—A Roman voluptuary at the court of Nero whose ambition was to shine as a court exquisite. He is generally supposed to be the author of certain fragments of a comic romance called *Petronii Arbitri Satyricon*.

[49]**Quintilian**, born in Spain 40 A.D. was a celebrated teacher of rhetoric and oratory at Rome. His great work is De *Institutione Oratorica*, a complete system of rhetoric, which is here referred to.

[50]**Longinus**, a Platonic philosopher and famous rhetorician, born either in Syria or at Athens about 213 A.D., was probably the best critic of antiquity. From his immense knowledge, he was called "a living library" and "walking museum," hence the poet speaks of him as inspired by *all the Nine*—Muses that is. These were Clio, the muse of History, Euterpe, of Music, Thaleia, of Pastoral and Comic Poetry and Festivals, Melpomene, of Tragedy, Terpsichore, of Dancing, Erato, of Lyric and Amorous Poetry, Polyhymnia, of Rhetoric and Singing, Urania, of Astronomy, Calliope, of Eloquence and Heroic Poetry.

[51]**Rome.**—For this pronunciation (to rhyme with *doom*) he has Shakespeare's example as precedent.

And the monks finished what the Goths begun.[52]

At length Erasmus, that great injured name[53]
(The glory of the priesthood and the shame!)
695   Stemmed the wild torrent of a barbarous age,
And drove those holy Vandals off the stage.[54]

But see! each muse, in Leo's golden days,[55]
Starts from her trance and trims her withered bays,
Rome's ancient genius o'er its ruins spread
700   Shakes off the dust, and rears his reverent head
Then sculpture and her sister arts revive,
Stones leaped to form, and rocks began to live;
With sweeter notes each rising temple rung,
A Raphael painted, and a Vida sung[56]
705   Immortal Vida! on whose honored brow
The poets bays and critic's ivy grow
Cremona now shall ever boast thy name
As next in place to Mantua, next in fame!

But soon by impious arms from Latium chased,
710   Their ancient bounds the banished muses passed.
Thence arts o'er all the northern world advance,
But critic-learning flourished most in France,

---

[52]**Goths.**—A powerful nation of the Germanic race, which, originally from the Baltic, first settled near the Black Sea, and then overran and took an important part in the subversion of the Roman empire. They were distinguished as Ostro Goths (Eastern Goths) on the shores of the Black Sea, the Visi Goths (Western Goths) on the Danube, and the Moeso Goths, in Moesia

[53]**Erasmus.**—A Dutchman (1467-1536), and at one time a Roman Catholic priest, who acted as tutor to Alexander Stuart, a natural son of James IV. of Scotland as professor of Greek for a short time at Oxford, and was the most learned man of his time. His best known work is his *Colloquia*, which contains satirical onslaughts on monks, cloister life, festivals, pilgrimages etc.

[54]**Vandals.**—A race of European barbarians, who first appear historically about the second century, south of the Baltic. They overran in succession Gaul, Spain, and Italy. In 455 they took and plundered Rome, and the way they mutilated and destroyed the works of art has become a proverb, hence the monks are compared to them in their ignorance of art and science.

[55]**Leo.**—Leo X., or the Great (1513-1521), was a scholar himself, and gave much encouragement to learning and art.

[56]**Raphael** (1483-1520), an Italian, is almost universally regarded as the greatest of painters. He received much encouragement from Leo. **Vida**—A poet patronised by Leo. He was the son of poor parents at Cremona (see line 707), which therefore the poet says, would be next in fame to Mantua, the birthplace of Virgil as it was next to it in place.

"Mantua vae miserae nimium vicina Cremona."—Virg.

The rules a nation born to serve, obeys;
And Boileau still in right of Horace sways[57]
But we, brave Britons, foreign laws despised,
715 And kept unconquered and uncivilized,
Fierce for the liberties of wit and bold,
We still defied the Romans as of old.
Yet some there were, among the sounder few
Of those who less presumed and better knew,
720 Who durst assert the juster ancient cause,
And here restored wit's fundamental laws.
Such was the muse, whose rule and practice tell[58]
"Nature's chief masterpiece is writing well."
Such was Roscommon, not more learned than good,[59]
725 With manners generous as his noble blood,
To him the wit of Greece and Rome was known,
And every author's merit, but his own
Such late was Walsh—the muse's judge and friend,[60]
Who justly knew to blame or to commend,
730 To failings mild, but zealous for desert,
The clearest head, and the sincerest heart,
This humble praise, lamented shade! receive,
This praise at least a grateful muse may give.
The muse whose early voice you taught to sing
735 Prescribed her heights and pruned her tender wing,
(Her guide now lost) no more attempts to rise,
But in low numbers short excursions tries,
Content if hence the unlearned their wants may view,
The learned reflect on what before they knew
740 Careless of censure, nor too fond of fame,
Still pleased to praise, yet not afraid to blame,
Averse alike to flatter, or offend,
Not free from faults, nor yet too vain to mend.

---

[57]**Boileau.**—An illustrious French poet (1636-1711), who wrote a poem on the Art of Poetry, which is copiously imitated by Pope in this poem.

[58]Refers to the Duke of Buckingham's *Essay on Poetry* which had been eulogized also by Dryden and Dr. Garth.

[59]**Roscommon**, the Earl of, a poet, who has the honor to be the first critic who praised Milton's *Paradise Lost*, died 1684.

[60]**Walsh.**—An indifferent writer, to whom Pope owed a good deal, died 1710.

Printed in Great Britain
by Amazon